Brian Moses lives in Sussex with his wife and two daughters. He travels the country performing his poems in schools and libraries. Before becoming a full-time writer, he worked as a teacher and can verify that everything in this book is true (well, almost!).

Lucy Maddison is a world-famous illustrator and has a secret life of her own. She lives in Balham, London, with her cat.

Tim Archbold was born at an early age and was abandoned by his parents at the age of thirty-eight. The art college he briefly attended is now a famous car park in Newcastle upon Tyne. His two children are convinced he is a bank manager, but he is always available to push them on a swing or drive them to a *Star Wars* birthday party.

THE SECRET LIVES OF TEACHERS

REVEALING RHYMES CHOSEN BY
BRIAN MOSES

ILLUSTRATED BY
LUCY MADDISON AND TIM ARCHBOLD

MACMILLAN CHILDREN'S BOOKS

Dedicated to the children and teachers I meet in the schools that I visit. And for all the children – and some teachers – who said good things about the first book. And for pupils and teachers at Little Ridge C.P. School, St Leonards-on-Sea.

The Secret Lives of Teachers first published 1996, *More Secret Lives of Teachers* first published 1997 and
The Top Secret Lives of Teachers first published in 2002

This edition published 2005 by Macmillan Children's Books
a division of Macmillan Publishers Limited
20 New Wharf Road, London N1 9RR
Basingstoke and Oxford
Associated companies throughout the world
www.panmacmillan.com

ISBN 978-0-330-43282-5

A CIP catalogue record for this book is available from
the British Library.

Printed and bound in Great Britain by Mackays of Chatham Ltd, Chatham, Kent

Secret Lives of Teachers

What Teachers Wear In Bed!

It's anybody's guess
what teachers wear in bed at night
so we held a competition
to see if any of us were right.

We did a spot of research,
although some of them wouldn't say,
but it's probably something funny
as they look pretty strange by day.

Our Headteacher's quite old-fashioned,
he wears a Victorian nightshirt,
our sports teacher wears her tracksuit
and sometimes her netball skirt.

That new teacher in the infants
wears bedsocks with see-through pyjamas,
our Deputy Head wears a T-shirt
he brought back from the Bahamas.

We asked our secretary what she wore
but she shooed us out of her room,
and our teacher said, her favourite nightie
and a splash of expensive perfume.

And Mademoiselle, who teaches French,
is really very rude,
she whispered, '*Alors!* Don't tell a soul,
but I sleep in the . . . back bedroom!'

Brian Moses

Ms Spry

Sweet Miss Spry
Seems rather shy,
But Ben and I
Think she's a spy,
Living in a shady dive
And being paid by MI5.

John Kitching

Do You Know My Teacher?

(female teacher version)

(fill in the word you think is most appropriate)

She's got a piercing stare and long black . . .
a) teeth
b) shoes
c) moustache
d) hair

She eats chips and beef and has short sharp . . .
a) doorstoppers
b) fangs
c) nails
d) teef

She is slinky and thin and has a pointed . . .
a) banana
b) chin
c) beard
d) umbrella

She has a long straight nose and hairy little . . .
a) kneecaps
b) ears
c) children
d) toes

John Rice

15

Miss Mooney

Miss Mooney's gone all moony,
not with-it anymore,
staring out the window,
looking at the floor.

Miss Mooney's gone all mopey,
there's a funny look in her eyes,
gazing up at the ceiling,
breathing hefty sighs.

We have a theory:
ever since he came,
that new Mr Pritchard,
she's not been the same!

Mind you, he is dishy,
and Class Three says he's fun . . .
lucky old Class Three then!
unlucky us Class One!

Miss Mooney's gone all gawpy,
in Poetry today
she read 'My Love Is Like a Red Red Rose':
what more is there to say!

Matt Simpson

Head Teacher Flips Her Lid

Look – there's the Head Teacher!
The one over there!
She's stormed from her office,
she's torn out her hair,
she's punching the door,
she's kicking the wall,
she's doing a head stand
on top of a stool,
she's doing a cart-wheel
in front of the class,
her eyes are all bloodshot,
her mouth's full of grass,
she's flinging her arms up,
she's beating her breast,
she's spray-canned the playground

'HEAD TEACHERS ARE BEST',
she's spray-canned
the front door,
she's spray-canned the wall
'HEAD TEACHER WOZ 'ERE'
and 'HEAD TEACHER IS COOL',
'HEAD TEACHER'S THE BRAINIEST
UNDER THE SUN',
'HEAD TEACHER IS GREAT –
SHE'S ACE, NUMBER ONE'.

head
teacher
woz
ere

She suddenly turns;
for what can she hear?
A very loud ringing
that's next to her ear.
She jumps when she sees
that she isn't alone:
her secretary's saying
'Oh, Head, it's the phone.'
She opens her eyes
with a throat-clearing cough:
'I think I was dreaming.

I must have dozed off.'

Charles Thomson

head
teachers
are
best

head
teacher
rules
O.K.

Through The Staffroom Door

Ten tired teachers slumped in the staffroom at playtime,
one collapsed when the coffee ran out, then there were nine.

Nine tired teachers making lists of things they hate,
one remembered playground duty, then there were eight.

Eight tired teachers thinking of holidays in Devon,
one slipped off to pack his case, then there were seven.

Seven tired teachers, weary of children's tricks,
one hid in the stock cupboard, then there were six.

Six tired teachers, under the weather, barely alive,
one gave an enormous sneeze, then there were five.

Five tired teachers, gazing at the open door,
one made a quick getaway, then there were four.

Four tired teachers, faces lined with misery,
one locked herself in the ladies, then there were three.

Three tired teachers, wondering what to do,
one started screaming when the bell rang, then there were two.

Two tired teachers, thinking life really ought to be fun,
one was summoned to see the Head, then there was one.

One tired teacher caught napping in the afternoon sun,
fled quickly from the staffroom, then there were none.

Brian Moses

Ms Sayer

Ms Sayer is lazy.
She hates waking up.
She loathes each new term.
She loves breaking up.

John Kitching

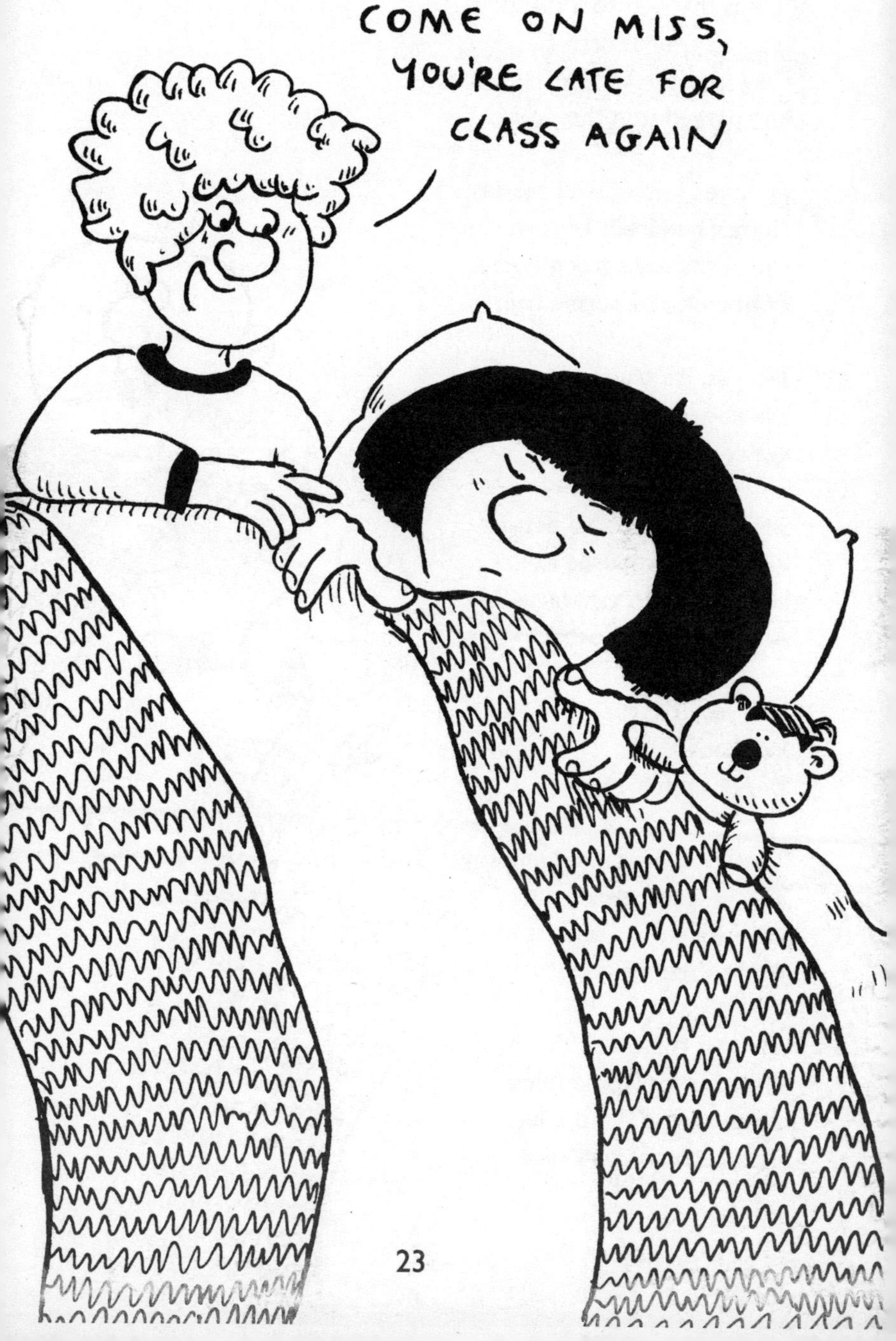
COME ON MISS, YOU'RE LATE FOR CLASS AGAIN

I Deliver Their Papers – So I Know

Miss is married to a Martian
I saw its friends arrive,
They flew the UFO up the road
And parked it in the drive.

She gives lots of wild parties;
There's hundreds of them there.
The aliens have green bodies
With pink and purple hair.

Yes, yes, it's true.
We know
We've seen it too.

Sir has got a special pet;
It's a Tyrannosaurus Rex.
He feeds it on asparagus
And abandoned ostrich eggs.

Yes, yes, it's true.
We know
We've seen it too.

The Head lives in a bungalow,
The garden's very neat,
His wife always says hello
And sometimes gives me sweets.

They've got two little children,
A cat, a dog, some mice.
I often see them playing;
They're really very nice.

You never saw that
With your own two eyes!
I don't believe it,
You're telling lies!

Trevor Millum

Our Dad Is A Teacher

Our dad is a teacher.
And if that's not bad enough,
he teaches in our school,
so we see both sides of him.

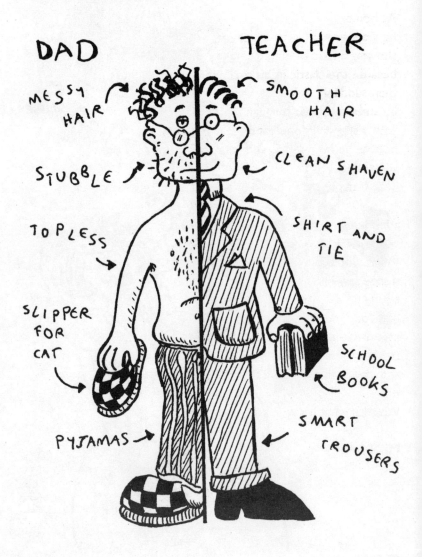

At school,
dad struts about importantly:
'don't run down the corridor'
tuck your shirt in boy'
'get your hands out of your pockets'
'don't you DARE let me hear that word again!'

At home,
he slobs around in the morning,
showing a load of bum cleavage
because the elastic in his pyjamas is going;
then suddenly,
he streaks topless through the kitchen
with a slipper in one hand
holding up his pyjamas with the other,
screaming
'that blanking cat is blanking on my blanking garden again'.

At school,
our dad is respected.
What would the kids think
if they saw him
sitting on the toilet
bathroom door open
pyjama trousers round his ankles
reading Michael Rosen poems
and singing like a Goon?

Wonder what it's worth to keep quiet?

Mike Jubb

I'M OFF!

Truants

Mr Flint drove to school each day
with Mrs Brice,
along the way they shared conversation,
shared their troubles, shared petrol money,
and then one day,
one warm bright day at the start of summer,
when the last thing they felt like doing
was teaching troublesome children,
they drove on,
right past the school gates.
Several children saw them,
several children waved
but they took no notice.
They drove on through towns and villages,
past cows and horses at rest on hillsides,
past a windmill, its sails turning lazily
until finally they could travel no more
and ahead of them stretched the sea.
Then they turned and looked at each other
and wondered what they'd done,
but as they'd driven such a long way,
they thought they might as well enjoy themselves.
So they paddled in the sea,
they skipped and chased along the beach,
they flipped stones into the water,
they built a magnificent sandcastle.
For lunch they ate ice cream and candyfloss.
Then they rode a miniature train
to the end of the pier and back,
played a double round of crazy golf,
lost lots of money in amusement arcades
and shared two bags of fish and chips
with a gang of gulls on the prom.

They drove home in silence,
past the horses and cows
and the windmill now still
past the school gates
now firmly locked for the night.

And when they sneaked back to school next day
all sheepish and shy,
embarrassed at the fuss they'd caused,
their headteacher
made them go outside at playtime
for a whole week!

Brian Moses

Things To Find In Teacher's Trouser Turn-ups

Just find any male member of staff
who wears trousers that have turn-ups
and you will usually find
that they have been wearing exactly the same pair
for years.
And years. And years.

Imagine what can be found in those turn-ups . . .
Crumbs from ancient sandwiches
Congealed curry stains
Fluff
A dead woodlouse
Flakes of chocolate
Cigarette ash
A paper clip
Bogies
Earwax that looks like yellow cheese
Yellow cheese that looks like earwax
More fluff.

Whatever you do,
if you decide to have a look for yourself
and they see you peering at their trousers
they'll suddenly get very embarrassed
go very red indeed
and check to see if their flies are undone.

Paul Cookson

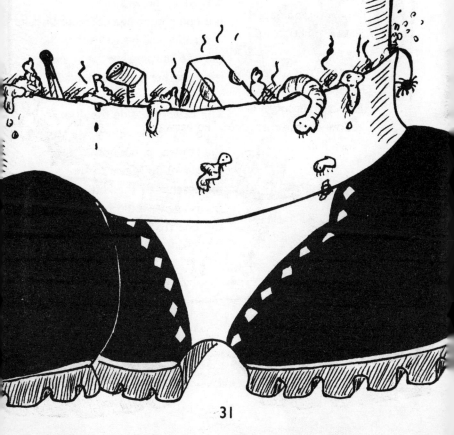

Tea

The teacher by the window
is thinking about class 4b,
the one reading the paper
is wishing she was rich,
the one chomping chocolate biscuits
is dreaming of his girlfriend,
the one slurping low-fat yoghurt
is hoping her car's been fixed.

The teacher beside the door
is hoping the knocking will stop,
the student in the corner
is wondering where to sit,
the teacher by the kettle
is wishing it would boil,
the one staring wearily at the wall
is thinking her head will split.

The teacher reading the notices
is not really thinking at all,
the one with her head in a magazine
is dreaming of sun and sea,
the one in the tie is rubbing his eyes
and hoping he's not going bald,
but the teacher by the window
is thinking about class 4b,

he's the one
who just spilt his tea.

Dave Calder

Be-Bop-A-Lula

Four of our teachers have formed
A POP GROUP!

Mr Holland is on keyboards
Miss Costello sings
Mr Clapton plays guitar
Mrs Collins bashes drums.

My dad says he saw them, once,
performing in a pub.
His opinion: Well, for a bunch of teachers,
they were really rather good.

Perhaps they'll make a record.
Have a hit
and then quit school?

Tour the world as superstars?
Become hip?
And rich? And cool!

Until then
they'll have to teach us
how to read and how to write.

Hang on
to their day jobs.
Perform their music late at night

And during breaks
(if they're not
on playground duty).

Be-Bop-A-lula a rock
classic which provided
legendary rock 'n' roller
Gene Vincent with his first
million-seller in 1956

Note: They still need a bass player.
Any volunteers?

('Be-Bop-A-Lula': a rock classic which provided legendary
rock'n'roller Gene Vincent with his first million-seller in 1956.)

Bernard Young

Extra-Money Activities (night-club)

Mr Count who teaches Maths,
became a comic just for laughs.

Behind the bar is Madame Drench
who by the day takes us for French.

Dinner lady, Mrs Kipper,
took the job as part-time stripper.

Mr Smart from Art and Craft
earns more for brushing floors. It's daft!

Miss Plummy-Tongue, of gentle breed,
who listens to us when we read,
at night is now attending to
the cloakroom and the ladies' loo.

German teacher, Herr von Frizz
compiles the local knowledge quiz.

Jack O'Toole, O'school caretaker,
got appointed as head waiter.

Mrs Note, the Music tutor's
ringing bells for 'TIME', in future.

(We hesitate . . . er . . . to announce . . . er . . .
the Head's applied to be a bouncer.)

Gina Douthwaite

School Report

Becky Sams
  told
    Jane Parkes
     who told
      Bee Moran
       who told Gail Pendry
       who told
        her cousin Karen
        who told
         Beth Lord
         who told
          Marilyn Cutts
          who told
           Maggie Dobbs
           who told
           Tracey Vine
           who told
           Val Clark
           who told

                    me

38

that she'd seen
Mr Pritchard & Miss Gibbs
holding hands
& choosing satsumas
together
in Sainsbury's
on Saturday.

I told you
there was something going on
between those two –
didn't I!

Tony Langham

The Lone Teacher

We've got a new teacher
he wears a mask
and a big wide hat.

He comes to school
on a silver horse
and rides around the field
all day.

Sometimes he says
'Have you seen Toronto?'

We tell him
we haven't been to Canada
but is it near
the Panama Canal
because we did that in geography
last term.

At four o'clock
he rides off into the sunset
and comes back the next morning
in a cloud of dust.

We wonder if
he will ever come and teach us Maths
like he said he would
when he first arrived.

Perhaps then he'll tell us his name
not keep it a secret
because my dad always asks me
'Who is that man?'

David Harmer

Bogeyman Headmaster

Our headmaster is a bogeyman
Our headmaster is a bogeyman
and he'll catch you if he can.

He creeps through the window
when the school is closed at night
just to give the caretaker a fright.

Our headmaster is a bogeyman
Our headmaster is a bogeyman
and he'll catch you if he can.

When he walks
his feet never touch the ground.
When he talks
his mouth never makes a sound.
That's why assembly is so much fun.

You should see him float through the air
when we say our morning prayer
and at assembly the teachers get trembly
when the piano starts to play on its own.
It's our bogeyman headmaster having a bogeyman joke.

Only the lollipop lady doesn't feel scared
'cause when he tried his bogeyman trick
she said, 'Buzz off or I'll hit you with my stick.'

Life can be lonely
for our bogeyman headmaster
but from his office you can always hear
this strange sound of laughter.

John Agard

Do You Know My Teacher?

(male teacher version)

(fill in the word you think is most appropriate)

He adores pork pies and has big blue . . .
a) legs
b) pencils
c) eyes
d) ears

MY VERY OWN PENCIL

YOU'RE NOT VERY TALL ARE YOU SIR?

He's not very tall in fact he's rather . . .
a) daft
b) old
c) bookish
d) small

He won't stand for any capers every day he reads the . . .
a) Beano
b) dictionary
c) papers
d) Corn Flakes packet

HOW VER INFORMATI

CORN FLAKES

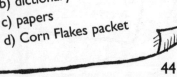

John Rice

45

Slander

We all talk about the teachers
and joke about the clothes they wear.
We all talk about the ones we like
and the ones that just aren't fair.

We all talk about the teachers,
the ones that scream and yell,
the ones that keep us in at break
and even some that smell!

We all talk about the teachers
and the stupid things they say,
the things that drive us bonkers
till we feel like running away.

But yesterday I crept to the staffroom
because I'd missed my bus.
And just you wait till I tell you
the things they were saying about us!

Tony Mitton

Where Do All The Teachers Go?

Where do all the teachers go
When it's 4 o'clock?
Do they live in houses
And do they wash their socks?

Do they wear pyjamas
And do they watch TV?
And do they pick their noses
The same as you and me?

Do they live with other people
Have they mums and dads?
And were they ever children
And were they ever bad?

Did they ever, never spell right
Did they ever makes mistakes?
Were they punished in the corner
If they pinched the chocolate flakes?

Did they ever lose their hymn books
Did they ever leave their greens?
Did they scribble on the desk tops
Did they wear old dirty jeans?

I'll follow one back home today
I'll find out what they do?
Then I'll put it in a poem
That they can read to you.

Peter Dixon

TEACHER TOWN

LIBRARY

BORING CLOTHES SHOP

SCHOOL DINNERS CAFE

SUMS STREET

BOOK SHOP

DETENTION DRIVE

BIOLOGY

BANDSTAND

KEEP OFF THE GRASS

REVISION ROAD

49

Deep, Dark, Strange And Nasty Secrets In The Staffroom

There are deep, dark, strange and nasty
secrets in the staffroom
when the teachers escape at break
from the confines of the classroom.
What's behind, what do we find
behind the staffroom door?
What lurks inside, what secrets hide
behind the staffroom door?

There are a thousand cups unfinished
all covered in green mould.
Coffee stains and rings remain
where they have overflowed.
Piles of files and unmarked books
and last term's lost reports,
the P.E. teacher's sweaty vest
and Lycra cycling shorts.

There are last week's lunch left-overs,
yoghurt pots and crusts,
banana skins and cola tins
all covered in chalk dust.
Examination papers
from nineteen sixty-eight
and the *Times Ed* job section
that's ten years out of date.

The ashtray's overflowed
and it's seeping out the door.
The wind has blown a million sheets
of paper on the floor.

There's paper planes and brown tea stains
from last night's staff meeting.
This place is a downright disgrace
not fit for a pig to eat in.

Inside the fridge half-finished milk
is lumpy and it's glowing.
The cartons are all starting
to mutate and they are growing.
The crockery mountain in the sink
is coated in green lime
and the room that time forgot
is left to rot in gunge and slime.

Beware the beings from this place,
the ones who always say
'No-one leaves this room
until this mess is cleared away!'
But if you said the same to them
one thing is very clear
to get the staffroom spick and span
would take them all a year
. . . or two . . . or three . . . or four

There are deep, dark, strange and nasty . . . etc.

Paul Cookson

51

Day Closure

We had a day closure on Monday
and I spent the morning in bed,
but the teachers went in as usual
and someone taught them instead.

And I thought of them all in the classroom,
stuck to their seats in rows,
some of them sucking pen lids,
Head Teacher scratching his nose.

Perhaps it's a bit like an MOT
to check if teachers still know
the dates of our kings and queens
or the capital of so and so.

Perhaps they had tables and spellings,
did the Head give them marks out of ten?
And then, if they got any wrong,
did he make them learn them again?

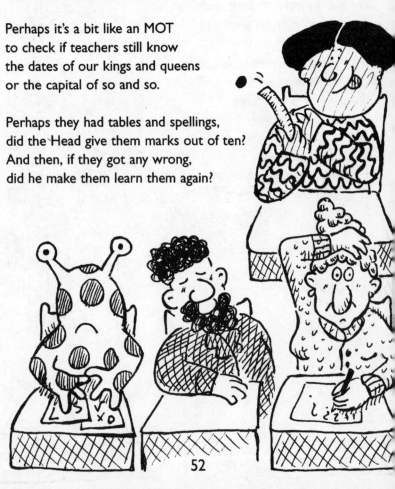

I thought of them out at break time
playing football or kiss chase or tag,
picking up teams in the playground
or scoffing crisps from a bag.

If I'd been a fly on the wall,
I might have watched while they slaved.
I'd have seen who asked silly questions
or if anyone misbehaved.

I thought of them all going home,
crossing the road to their mums.
They looked very grim the next day.
It couldn't have been much fun.

Brian Moses

Gentle, Sweet And Deadly

We always thought that our RE teacher
Was a kind and gentle lady –
Her voice was soft, and her eyes were kind.
Yes, a sweet little thing was Miss Brady.

But on Saturday, boy, did we get a shock,
We couldn't believe it was true –
Little Miss Brady had a weekend job
as a wrestler called 'Slippery Sue'!

PUT ME DOWN!

A female wrestler! Little Miss Brady,
Who teaches forgiveness and peace –
Dressed in a leotard, yellow and blue,
And covered all over in grease.

She's half the size of all the others,
But because she's greasy and small
She always slips out of all of their holds,
They can't pin her down in a fall.

We saw her there, as real as can be,
On 'Saturday Sport' on the telly,
Grabbing opponents by hair and by throat,
And butting 'em all in the belly.

The crowd went wild, they chanted her name –
'Slippery, Slippery Sue.'
And there was Miss Brady, larger than life
In the ring, on the telly – it's true!
We still can't believe it's little Miss Brady –
To think how she's fooled folk for years.
Instead of just orange juice, coffee or tea
She prob'ly downs twenty-odd beers!

But now that we know, there's one thing for sure –
If we get told off by Miss Brady,
You can bet your life there'll be no back-chat –
You just can't mess with that lady.

Clive Webster

Secret

'Hey, Katie, I have something to tell you!'

'What's that?'

'I found out when I got pulled up for talking.'

'Go on then.'

'You know that Sir put me outside the classroom.'

'So what?'

'Well, that was when I saw them! They were walking . . .'

'Saw who?'

'Along the corridor outside the Maths room.'

'Oh, yeah?'

'You should have seen my face! I just sat gawping!'

'At what?'

'They never saw me, though. I kept my head down.'

'Well, tell me!'

'They held hands and her head was on his shoulder!'

'What next?'

They stopped outside the Maths room door and turned round.'

'Yes, but who?'

'Face to face, and gazing at each other.'

'Tell me, do!'

'He kissed her and she had her arms around . . .'

'For Heaven's sake!'

'His neck! I'll have to run or I'm in bother.'

'Wait, not yet!'

'I'll tell you, but promise it's a secret – '

'Yes, yes!'

'Crikey! There's the bell – I'll have to hurry'.

'I promise!'

'Don't tell anybody else I leaked it!'

'I can't hear you!'

'Miss Lavine's in love with Mr Murray.'

'SPEAK UP!'

'MISS LAVINE'S IN LOVE WITH MR MURRAY!'

Elizabeth Carr

57

Not Five But Seven Days A Week

Next weekend go into town
And spot the teachers all around,
They're out there practising what they preach
Not five but *seven* days a week.

They just don't get it, that they're free
For two whole days, just as they please,
Instead they're marching up and down,
Still on duty, armed with frown.

On passers-by they like to pounce –
'How many grammes are in an ounce?'
'How many Ss in Mississippi?'
'Mind your language – don't get lippy!'

Tired shoppers can't believe the fuss –
'There'll be no talking on this bus!'
'No pushing in the check-out queue
And hands up if you want the loo.'

'No running in supermarket aisles,
Get shopping stacked in tidy piles,
No eating sweets or chewing gum,
And don't be cheeky to your mum.'

Still later when the streets have emptied,
And to their homes they can't be tempted,
You see these teachers – completely bats –
Talking multiplication with alley cats.

Jane Wright

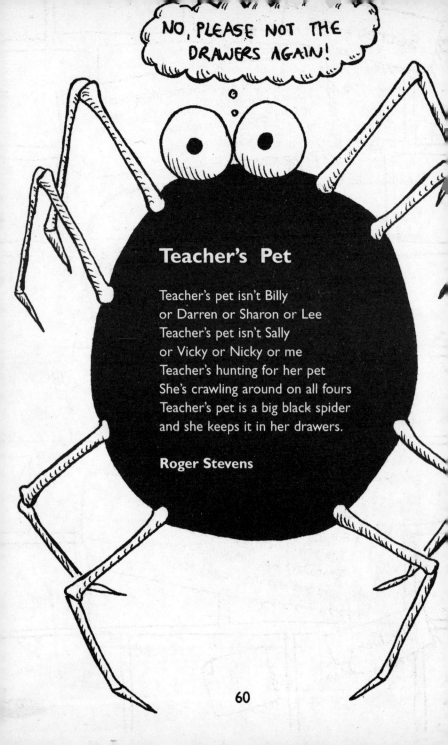

Teacher's Pet

Teacher's pet isn't Billy
or Darren or Sharon or Lee
Teacher's pet isn't Sally
or Vicky or Nicky or me
Teacher's hunting for her pet
She's crawling around on all fours
Teacher's pet is a big black spider
and she keeps it in her drawers.

Roger Stevens

Secret Love

Chalked on a wall in the playground,
These words inside a heart:
'David loves Susan forever,
And we shall never part.'

David loves Susan
forever
and we shall
never part

But nobody knew, and nobody guessed,
The secret behind what it said:
That Dave was the History teacher,
And Sue was the Deputy Head.

Mike Jubb

Our Hippy Teacher

Miss Thomson's vague and dreamy
and given half a chance,
   will meditate through lessons
      and end up in a trance.

   We think she's been a hippy
      as she strongly favours beads.
      Her clothes are psychedelic
         and she makes baskets out of reeds.

   And if you gaze too closely
      in her vague and dreamy eyes
      you discover to your cost
         she has the power to hypnotize.

      'You will obey,' she murmurs.
      'You will study till you drop
      and not until I clap
      are you allowed to stop.'

      And then she puts her feet up
         with a mild, contented smirk
   and dreams away till hometime
   while we do all the work.

   Marian Swinger

Escape Route

When our teacher came to school today
he looked bright and happy, not old and grey,
not the usual bear whose head was sore,
and we hadn't seen him like this before.
He parked his car in our headteacher's space,
you should have seen the look on her face
as she swept like a hurricane into our room,
and it brightened up our Monday gloom.
But instead of looking a picture of worry
or smiling nervously and saying sorry
he'd go out and shift it straightaway,
our teacher told her that from today
she could stay and teach his class,
and the look on her face was like frosted glass.
He ripped up test papers in front of her eyes,
then jumped up and down, and to our surprise
planted a slobbery kiss on her cheek
and just for a moment she couldn't speak
till he told us how on Saturday night
his lottery numbers had all been right.
Then a noise from outside made us all look round
as a helicopter landed in our school grounds,
and our teacher said, 'It's my taxi at last,
this school, all of you, are now in my past.'
Then while we watched, the big blades whirred
and he left for the sky as free as a bird.

And his car is still parked in our headteacher's space.
You should have seen the look on her face!

Brian Moses

The I-Spy Book of Teachers

One point if you catch your teacher yawning,
double that to two if later on you find him snoring,
Three points if you hear your teacher singing

and four if it's a pop song not a hymn.
A generous five points if you ever see him jogging
and six if you should chance upon him snogging.

Seven if you ever find him on his knees and praying
for relief from noisy boys who trouble him.
Eight if you should catch him in the betting shop,

nine if you see him dancing on *Top of the Pops*,
And ten if you hear him say what a lovely class he's got
for then you'll know there's something wrong with him.

Brian Moses

The Teacher's Curse

'Hateful pupils,' muttered Mrs Pye.
'Beastly, cheeky, lazy little brats.
Stand up that child who hit me in the eye.
Arise, foul missile thrower, like a man.'

Headmaster Jones popped in and shook his head.
'Disgraceful! Mrs Pye, control your class.'
He slammed the door and Mrs Pye blushed red.
'Revenge,' she muttered, raising high her arms.

The room grew dark, the pupils pale with fright
as Mrs Pye, her eyes a ghastly green,
cried, 'I, Tallora, Mistress of the Night,
call down upon your heads this awful curse.'

The children sat transfixed, with bated breath.
Tallora chanted, 'Teachers you shall be.
A fitting curse, a fate far worse than death.
And now, farewell sweet pupils, I depart.'

And, gliding to the door, Tallora went.
And pupils tittered, but it all came true.
Some now teach in Essex, some in Kent
and some of them could well be teaching you!

Marian Swinger

Hands

Last Saturday, shopping with my mum down town,
I caught a glimpse of Mrs Brown.
She must be 50 if she's a day.
Her face is wrinkled
And she's gone quite grey.
She's very old fashioned,
Wears blacks and blues,
Thick, thick stockings
And granny-type shoes.
But imagine, if you can,
My huge surprise.
I hardly could believe my eyes.
There she was, in the Saturday street,
Just as usual, greyly neat,
But walking along arm in arm
And holding the hand
Of a rock star from my favourite band.

And then I tell you
(I nearly missed it)
He took her hand
And gently kissed it!

And then my mum whispered
In a voice that just carried,
'But didn't you know
Those two are married?
Mrs Brown's been married to him for years.'
I hardly could believe my ears.
Who would have thought
Rock stars could ever have wives –
Or that teachers could ever
Have such secret lives?

John Kitching

71

Whispers of Love

Janis Priestley

73

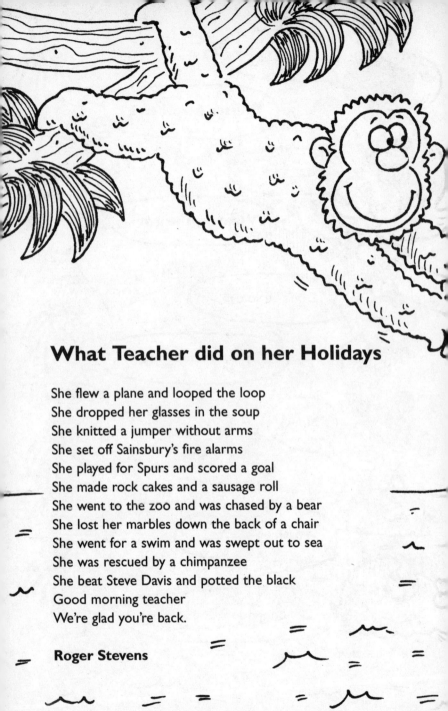

What Teacher did on her Holidays

She flew a plane and looped the loop
She dropped her glasses in the soup
She knitted a jumper without arms
She set off Sainsbury's fire alarms
She played for Spurs and scored a goal
She made rock cakes and a sausage roll
She went to the zoo and was chased by a bear
She lost her marbles down the back of a chair
She went for a swim and was swept out to sea
She was rescued by a chimpanzee
She beat Steve Davis and potted the black
Good morning teacher
We're glad you're back.

Roger Stevens

Love has an Effect on our Teacher

When our teacher fell in love with a doctor
She was ill every day of the week
When she fell in love with a plumber
Her radiator sprang a leak
When she fell in love with a dustman
She put her bin out every day
When she fell in love with a farmer
She spent the weekends baling hay
When she fell for a librarian
She was always borrowing books
When she fell in love with a policeman
She went chasing after crooks.

But when another teacher
Took our teacher's attention
They got married straight away
And kept each other in detention.

John Coldwell

Our Dad's the Deputy Head Now

Our dad's the Deputy Head now;
The kids all think he's hateful.
At least we've moved to a different school,
For which we are 'truly grateful'.
They say he's more bossy than ever,
Now that he's got more clout;
He stalks along the corridors
And puts some stick about.

'What do you think *you're* doing?
Wipe that smile off your face;
Who do you think you're talking to?
You're an absolute disgrace!'

At home, Dad's the same as ever.
The kids would have a laugh
If they saw him in Mum's pink shower cap
When he's singing in the bath.
At night, he goes out in the garden
For what he calls 'self-defence';
He picks up slugs and throws them
Over next door's garden fence.
When Mum told him off for it,
He snapped, 'I beg your pardon,
I'm paying them back for what their cat
Keeps doing in my garden.'

At school, our dad is the Deputy Head
He stands for Law and Order.
At home, he doesn't know yet:
We've been using his camcorder!

Mike Jubb

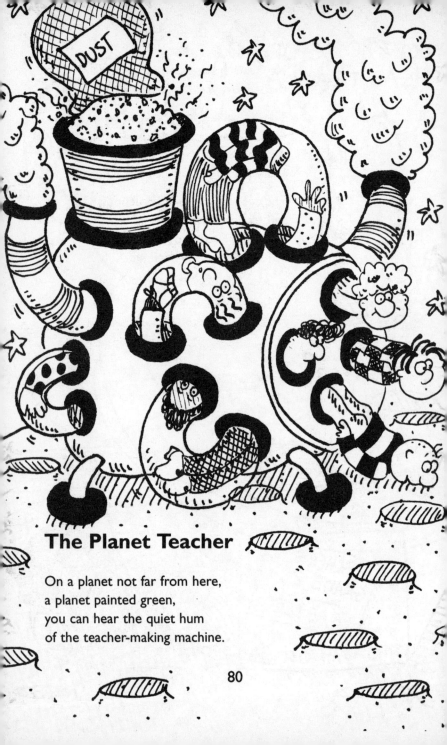

The Planet Teacher

On a planet not far from here,
a planet painted green,
you can hear the quiet hum
of the teacher-making machine.

For teachers are not born,
they're not like you or me.
No, teachers are made from dust
then given away for free.

They're packed in big brown boxes
with a coffee cup at the back,
two packets of smart red pens
and a National Curriculum pack.

They come with full instructions
and trousers that never fit,
and half a dozen odd socks
from a special odd-sock kit.

And finally they're wrapped
in coloured bits of straw,
before being dropped, on demand,
through someone's staffroom door.

Andrew Collett

I Think my Teacher is a Cowboy

It's not just
That she rides to school on a horse
And carries a Colt 45 in her handbag.

It's not just
the way she walks;
hands hanging over her hips.

It's not just
the way she dresses;
stetson hat and spurs on her boots.

It's not just the way she talks;
calling the playground the corral,
    the Head's room the Sheriff's office,
    the school canteen the chuck wagon,
    the school bus the stage coach,
    the bike sheds the livery stable.

What gives her away
Is when the hometime pips go.
She slaps her thigh
And cries
'Yee ha!'

John Coldwell

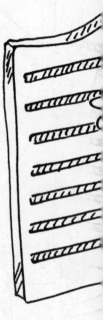

82

The Busy Head

ZOOOM!

There goes the Head —
he's off like a rocket —
each eye like a Catherine wheel
revolving in its socket.

WHIZZ!

Superman can't touch him
as he whizzes round the school —
up and down the corridor
and in and out the hall —

ZIP!

all about the playground
and then upon the stage
with the vigour of a tiger
escaping from a cage.

SCOOT!

He breaks the speed of sound
with a supersonic blast
and there's just a flash of light
to say the Head's gone past.

He's the busiest person
in the school, it's true,
but there's one thing that I wonder –
what exactly does he do?

Charles Thomson

85

Circumstantial Evidence

Mr Tramain, our science teacher, is a space alien.
For a start he's much too old to be human –
'*Two hundred!*' he irritably let slip when I asked.

Also he's telepathic – when he says
'*I know what you're up to, boy!*'
He's always right.

Sometimes when he's teaching he forgets to speak our tongue,
Just drones on in some scientific language
So that we've no idea what he's on about.

Once he told us he was interested in astronomy –
Said he had a telescope at home to gaze at the stars,
Just suffers from homesickness I bet!

His wife's called Zara, or some such, and their kid is Zak –
Alien names if ever I've heard them –
And he's admitted they come from somewhere *far away*.

In last year's pantomime
He appeared as the not-very-jolly green giant –
I bet he just *removed* his make-up for that part.

But what absolutely convinces me
(I must warn our headmaster Mr Greenman-Little)
Is I've just rearranged the letters in Tramain!

Philip Waddell

Postcard from the Edge

Dear Class_____(fill in year)
I'm having ☐ a wonderful time ☐ sweet dreams of you
☐ a nervous breakdown.
We arrived after sixteen ☐ hours ☐ days ☐ Hell's Angels
helped us fix our flat tyre.
Still, the hotel is ☐ atop a huge cliff ☐ sliding over the cliff
☐ not built yet
and the views over ☐ the sea ☐ the bins ☐ Tesco's car park
are staggering.
I'd like to ☐ take in the sea air ☐ teach the world to sing
☐ strangle every one of you personally
but the doctor says ☐ I should take it easy ☐ I'm a raving loony
☐ I need help.
You mustn't think ☐ I don't miss you ☐ I like you
☐ because it hurts your head.
But I must admit taking this holiday is exactly
☐ what I needed ☐ what you needed ☐ what the rest of the
staff needed.
I know that little chemistry experiment was
☐ an accident ☐ an act of genius ☐ an act of sabotage
and that you didn't mean ☐ for it to happen ☐ to blow up the
school ☐ to set my cardigan on fire.

Auntie June ☐ is looking after me very well ☐ is sick of the sight of me ☐ has fallen in love with one of the Hell's Angels and says I should be up and about by ☐ next week ☐ next Christmas ☐ the time she counts to three
otherwise ☐ she'll have to get the doctor back ☐ she'll shout for Uncle Alfie ☐ there'll be trouble.
See you ☐ soon I hope ☐ not if I see you first ☐ in court.
Your ☐ loving ☐ demented ☐ redundant teacher,
_____(sign here).

Jane Wright

Sir's a Secret Agent

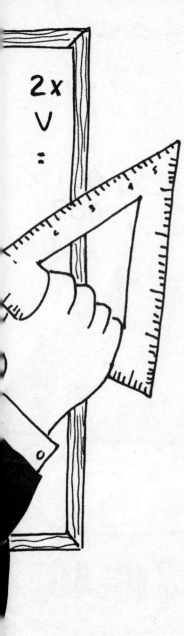

Sir's a secret agent
He's licensed to thrill
At Double-Oh Sevening
He's got bags of skill.

He's tall, dark and handsome
With a muscular frame
Teaching's his profession
But Danger's his game!

He's cool and he's calm
When he makes a decision
He's a pilot, sky-diver
And can teach long-division.

No mission's too big
No mission's too small
School-kids, mad scientists
He takes care of them all.

He sorts out the villains
The spies and the crooks
Then comes back to school
And marks all our books!

Tony Langham

Briggsy

It's her birthday.
She doesn't want anyone to know.
She's not intending to celebrate
hitting the big 4 0.

Yes, today Mrs Briggs is forty.
You can't tell. It doesn't show.
(And even if you think it does
don't you dare say so.)

Because TODAY MRS BRIGGS IS FORTY
and she doesn't want anyone to know.

Although,
when someone in class has a birthday
she announces it
and makes a big fuss

so

we'd like to make a big fuss of Mrs Briggs.
We've written a poem for her.
(We're planning to perform it in assembly.)

It goes like this:

Mrs Briggs you're forty
That's quite an age to reach

Mrs Briggs you're forty
Long may you teach

Mrs Briggs you're forty
You don't want a fuss

Mrs Briggs you're forty
Your secret's safe with us

CONGRATULATIONS MRS BRIGGS ON TURNING 40

It's called *Mrs Briggs You're Forty*
and we hope she likes it.

Bernard Young

93

Romance

I know there's something going on
between Mr Phipps and Miss White.
I've seen them in the car park,
how they linger when they say goodnight.

I caught them once in the TV room
with all of the blinds drawn down.
He said that he'd lost his glasses,
I bet they were fooling around.

When she wafts into our classroom
and catches him by surprise,
nothing is too much trouble,
there's a faraway look in his eyes.

Quite what she sees in him,
none of us really knows:
She's quite fashion conscious,
he wears some terrible clothes.

We think he sends her notes:
Please tick if you really love me,
and if she's slow to reply
We've seen him get awfully angry.

But when they're lovey-dovey,
He's just like a little boy,
cracking jokes and smiling again,
filling our class with his joy.

Brian Moses

The Excuse

She walked in nervously, biting her lip;
Trembling slightly, she could not meet their gaze.
'WELL?' shouted the class together –
Startled, the teacher made for the desk where
Behind the relative security of four wooden legs and
a jar of fading daisies
She felt an explanation coming on.
'WHERE'S OUR HOMEWORK?' yelled the class.
'Erm, well,' said the teacher, 'I haven't got it with me.'
'A LIKELY STORY,' sneered the class.
'YOU HAVEN'T DONE IT, HAVE YOU?' chorused the class.
'YOU HAVEN'T EVEN BOTHERED TO MARK OUR
    HOMEWORK!' they cried.
Inside her head she scrabbled desperately for something
    believable,
Sweat trickling down her temple and inside her palms.
'I dropped it getting off the bus. It landed
in a puddle then a
Huge gang of teachers took it off me and said
I wouldn't be let into the Staffroom Coffee-Tea Rotation
    Posse if I did it.
"Marking homework is for wimps," they said,' she said sadly,
a big round tear rolling slowly down her cheek.
'OH,' said the class, shifting uncomfortably,
'WELL, JUST MAKE SURE YOU HAVE IT FOR TOMORROW.
THERE, THERE. NO NEED TO CRY.'
'Thank you, class,' sniffed the teacher, brightening a little,
'It won't happen again, I promise.'

Jane Wright

The Amorous Teacher's Sonnet to His Love

Each morning I teach in a daze until
the bell that lets me hurry down and queue
with pounding heart to wait for you to fill
my eyes with beauty and my plate with stew.
Dear dinner lady, apple of my eye,
I long to shout *I love you* through the noise
and take your hand across the shepherd's pie
despite the squealing girls or snickering boys.
O let us flee together and start up
a little café somewhere in the Lakes
and serve day trippers tea in china cups
and buttered scones on pretty patterned plates.

Alas for dreams so rudely bust in two –
some clumsy child's spilt custard on my shoe.

Dave Calder

How to Look After a Teacher

Don't cross him on Monday morning
before he's quite awake;
if you want a peaceful classroom
keep out of his way at break.
(If you must thump Jamie,
do it round the corner.)

Always offer a sweet or crisp –
especially when eating in class;
admire his chronic taste in clothes
if you don't want extra maths.
(Perhaps he really likes
flared jeans with orange socks.)

Don't ask if he's wearing a wig today –
you'll only make him sore.
When he starts to say 'When I was at school . . .'
don't add, 'In the Boer War!'
(He can't really help being
an old man of thirty.)

Judith Nicholls

The Very Worst Thing of All

If you see
your mum and dad holding hands
it's embarrassing.

If you catch them
plant even the slightest peck on the cheek
it's dreadful.

If your mum
kisses you when you get out of the car
in front of everyone at school
it's awful.

If Darren the Slob and Dean the Blob
chase you around the yard
and try to kiss you
it's so revolting
you are sick for days.

But if you go to the pictures
with your best friend Julie
and just as the lights go down
as you begin to guzzle popcorn
you see Mr Evans, your class teacher,
slip a long and snaky arm
round the shoulders of Miss Carter,
who is of course your other teacher,
it really is the worst thing in the world.

It makes you go all red and burning
it makes you fizz and gasp
it makes your toenails tingle
it makes your stomach tremble
and you and Julie giggle
very loudly.

Of course
it's even worse for them
when they turn round
and see you.

David Harmer

HEAD TEACHER

The Dragon

Why do they call her 'The Dragon',
our fiery head teacher, Miss Quail?
    She's really quite nice,
    though she's told me off twice
when I've swung on a dangerous rail.

She can't help her big flaring nostrils –
great holes at the end of her snout.
    I'm sure it's a joke –
    must be cigarette smoke
that we sometimes see billowing out.

They say that the walls in her study
have claw marks right up to the ceiling.
    But some little twits
    drive her out of her wits,
so she must get a desperate feeling.

But why do they call her 'The Dragon'?
It seems so unfair to Miss Quail.
    She's normal to me –
    well, from what I can see
of her arms and her legs . . . and her tail!

Barry Buckingham

A Televised Surprise

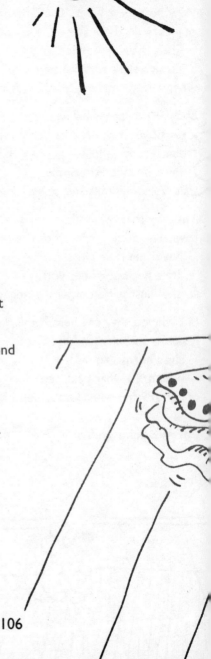

Imagine our delight
Consternation and surprise
Our teacher on *Come Dancing*
Right before our eyes.

She wore a dress of sequins
That glittered like a flight
Of silent, silver snowflakes
On a winter's night.

She really looked fantastic
No one could ignore
The magic of her dancing
Across the ballroom floor.

Her partner, tall and smart,
Only saw him from the back,
His hair was slicked down short
His suit and shoes were black.

He whirled and twirled her round
As the music got much faster
And then faced the camera
It was our Headmaster!

They seemed to dance for ever
Until it wasn't fun
And the competition stopped
The pair of them had won.

David Harmer

107

My Dad the Headmaster

My dad the Headmaster knows every single rule
and when he is at home he thinks that he's at school.
He rings the bell each morning and I'd better not be late
so I'm washed and down for breakfast at exactly ten to eight.

He stands and takes the register, checks my shirt and tie,
then he says 'Good Morning' and I have to reply
'Good–Mor–ning–Fa–ther' in that monotone drone
and hear his assembly in my very own home.

He has a list of rules that are pasted on each door:
No Spitting. No Chewing. No Litter On The Floor.
No Music. No Jewellery. No Make-Up. No Telly.
No Making Rude Noises Especially If They're Smelly.

No Videos. No Football. No Coloured Socks Or Laces.
No Trainers. No Jeans. No Smiling Faces.
No Sticking Bubble Gum In Your Sister's Hair.
No Wiping Bogies Down The Side Of The Chair.

He has a list of sayings for all types of occasion
and a set of phrases for every situation:
'Don't run down the stairs. Speak when spoken to.
Put your hand up first if you want to use the loo.

'I don't mind how long I wait. Listen when I'm speaking.
No one leaves the table until we've finished eating.
Don't interrupt and don't answer back.
Don't do this and don't do that.'

Yes, my dad the Headmaster knows every single rule
and when he is at home he thinks that he's at school.
But I am not the only one who does what he is told.
Dad never complains if his dinner is cold.

He's ever so polite when mother is around
and mumbles 'Yes my dear' while looking at the ground.
Her foghorn commands, they really drive him crazy.
Dad's scared stiff of Mum . . . she's a dinner lady!

Paul Cookson

Strange Supply

The work was out and ready.
The room was spick and span.
We all trooped in and took our seats
and the register began.

Our names were called in order.
All of us answered, 'Here!'
Uneasily we waited
for a teacher to appear.

But no one paced the classroom,
or none that we could see.
Only a voice rapped, 'Silence!
Now listen well to me.

'Ms Jones has leave of absence.
I shall not tell you why.
All you need know is simply this:
I am today's Supply.

'You need not seek to see me.
Be sure that I am here,
hovering at your elbow
or hissing in your ear.'

Throughout the day an awful hush
hung on our fearful class.
Our timid pencils crept along
as we prayed for time to pass.

Nobody made a murmur.
Nobody said a thing.
But all of us breathed a sigh when the final
bell began to ring.

So when next day the rumour spread,
'She's back! Ms Jones is here . . . !'
as she stepped through the door,
   the whole of class four
gave one almighty cheer.

Tony Mitton

The Swivel-hipped Kid

Our Music teacher was right old-fashioned –
His name was Mr Sidney.
He went on and on about classical stuff
So we called him 'Sidney Stravinsky'.

'Classical this' and 'classical that',
He rubbished anything pop.
He said that Tchaikovsky and Mozart and such
Was better than soul, rap or rock.

And yet Sid Stravinsky, old-fashioned and quiet
With his minim and crotchet and quaver,
And Schubert and Brahms and a fella called Grieg
Was really a right little raver.

I found out his secret merely by chance
At a club on our caravan site –
They have different things on throughout the week
And Thursday was 'New Talent Nite'.

We'd gone there and found ourselves seats near the front
And the show started off with a swing –
Two or three people just having a laugh
And trying their hardest to sing.

And then came the bombshell; the compere announced,
'And now folks, we've got Swinging Sid.
So let's hear it now, let's give a big hand
For Sid, the Swivel-hipped Kid.'

And old Sid Stravinsky was there in the flesh
With wig and electric guitar,
Shouting and yelling and jumping around
Like an ageing demented pop star.

Old Mr Sidney, who rubbished pop music,
Who was really old-fashioned and quiet,
Was there, like a madman, frantic on stage,
Screaming and starting a riot.

I couldn't believe it, honest I couldn't,
It was just as though I was dreaming –
My music teacher up there on the stage,
Gyrating and yelling and screaming.

And not only that, he came out the winner,
Through to the final no less,
Gyrating and yelling and screaming and such,
Honest, I'd never have guessed.

But I'll give the 'Kid' a nasty surprise,
At the final down there in September –
I'll get up a coachload of kids from our school
For a night he's going to remember.

He'll never again rubbish rap, rock or soul,
The old hypocrite wouldn't dare –.
He knows that we'd all just cry out in one voice,
'Hey Swivel-hipped Kid, WE WERE THERE!!!'

Clive Webster

The PE Teacher Wants to Be Tarzan

The PE teacher sits and dreams
Of swinging through the trees,
Of taking jungle holidays
And crushing pythons with his knees.

Of running off with nice Miss Jones
The new biology teacher.
Of taking her to a posh tree-house
Where no one else can reach her.

Instead he puffs and pants all day
In a drab and dreary gym,
And wishes that there were a spell
For liberating him.

Brian Patten

Miss Rose Lee

Monday – boring

Tuesday – boring

Wednesday – boring

Thursday – amazing!

On Thursday Miss Rose Lee,
Pirouetted through the door,
A rose between her teeth,
She spun across the floor,
And when she'd swung from beam to beam,
And danced across the ceiling,
She vanished through the skylight,
And left the whole class reeling.
'Where are you going, Miss?' called Pip,
But she simply didn't hear,
'She's off to join the circus,'
Whispered Billy in my ear,
'She's going to fly the high trapeze,
If I am not mistaken,
It's the last we'll see of Miss Rose Lee,
As sure as Pig is bacon.'

Friday – boring.

Mary Green

The Head's Hideout

The Head crouched in his hideout
Beneath a dustbin lid.
'I want to see,' he muttered,
'No teacher and no kid,

No parent, no inspector,
Never a district nurse,
And, please, not one school dinner:
The things are getting worse!'

All morning, as the phone rang,
He hid away. Instead;
'The Head is in the dustbin,'
The secretary said.

'The *Head* is in the *dustbin*?'
'Yes, he'll be there all day.
He likes sometimes to manage
A little getaway.

Last year he went to Holland.
Next year he's off to France.
Today he's in the dustbin.
You have to take your chance.'

The Head sprang from the garbage
As end-of-school came round.
He cried, 'That's quite the nastiest
Hideaway I've found!

I think I'll stick to teachers
And kids and parents too.
It's just sometimes I've had enough.'
Don't blame him. Do you?

Kit Wright

The Secret Life of Mr Harper

At school he's just the coolest teacher
Dressed in his designer best
The mums all think he's really great
The dads are not impressed.

He knows about the latest bands
And all Playstation Games
Knows everything on Pokemon,
Can tell you all their names.

Yes, Mr Harper's ace
Mr Harper's cool
Wicked, hip and up to date
The coolest guy in school.

But see him at the weekend
Down the railway station
You won't believe your eyes
At the transformation.

A knitted blue-and-yellow scarf
An orange large kagoul
A pair of flares, brown corduroy . . .
He doesn't seem so cool.

A duffle bag that's stuffed with crisps
A pair of thick rimmed glasses
Binoculars for peering at
Any train that passes.

A thousand pens for writing down
The numbers in his jotter,
Mr Harper's secret . . .
He's really a trainspotter.

Paul Cookson

Down in Sir's Cellar

Down in Sir's cellar where no one can see him,
Mr McDougal dances and sings.
He boils up a saucepan as big as a bucket
Filled with the weirdest, the strangest of things.

Gooey black treacle, brown ale and marmalade,
Baby oil, lemon juice, Tandoori paste.
He stirs and he stirs as it bubbles and splutters,
This fantastic mixture he doesn't dare taste.

Shiny glass jars are ready and waiting.
In goes a steaming hot, sludgy green batch
Of Mr McDougal's top-secret potion,
His own special remedy for his bald patch.

Patricia Leighton

Staff Meeting

The teachers have gathered in private to talk
About their collections of leftover chalk –
Bits that are rare, bits they just like,
And fragments they've saved just in case there's a
  strike.

One has a blue that you don't often see,
Another a remnant from nineteen-o-three.
They've thousands of pieces of boxes and tins,
Each sorted and counted with tweezers and pins.
And when all their best bits have been on display,
They'll take them home carefully, and lock them
away.

Nick Toczek

Teachers' Features

Do your teachers have strange features?
Then try this little game,
And as you read this poem
Just fill in the teacher's name!

_ _ _ wears her glasses on the tip of her long nose.
_ _ _ _ wears a toupee, but he doesn't think
        it shows.
_ _ wears so much make-up you can hardly
        see her face.
_ _ _ _ 's fashion sense is really a disgrace.

_ _ _ is always blinking,
_ _ _ _ keeps on winking,
_ _ _ has got a twitch,
_ _ _ looks like a witch.

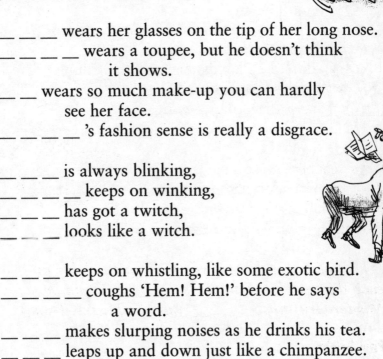

_ _ _ keeps on whistling, like some exotic bird.
_ _ _ _ coughs 'Hem! Hem!' before he says
        a word.
_ _ _ makes slurping noises as he drinks his tea.
_ _ _ leaps up and down just like a chimpanzee.

__ __ is always shouting,
__ __ is always pouting,
__ __ walks with a wiggle,
__ __ can't help but giggle.

__ __ __ waves his arms around like windmills
         in the air
__ __ __ won't do anything that might disturb
         her hair
__ __ __ think he's handsome, and the trouble
         is – he's right.
__ __ __ has a face to give you
         nightmares late at night.

Your teachers must have features
That aren't mentioned in my list
So why not write a poem
About all the ones I've missed!

*(This poem reads best if you have one syllable on
each dash so, for example, __ __ __ __ could be
Mis-ter-Griff-iths; __ __ __ could be Miss-Wil-son.)*

Paul Bright

127

New Teacher

Green hair sticking up
Short skirt
Crop top
Belly-button pierced (twice)
Old of course
But still quite nice
Says if we behave like angels
While the OFSTED are in school
She'll let us see her tattoo
Cool

Frances Nagle

Top Secret

TOP SECRET CATALOGUE
Teachers' Survival Guide
(it's for teachers' eyes only)
And we can supply worldwide!

Rear-view contact lenses
or wide-angle glasses –
they make all-round surveillance
possible in classes!

New! Space-age gadget!
(The technology's top-notch!)
you can track pupils' movements
with our satellite-linked watch!

Our hand-crafted button
conceals with its shape,
a strong long bungee-jump cord
for emergency escape!

Browse through all our booklets!
Latest titles include,
Legal Brutal Punishments,
How to Keep Your Class Subdued.

Order now for Spring Term,
and qualify to buy
for just HALFPRICE, our great new
book, *My Teacher Is a Spy!*

Liz Brownlee

Miss Drak: Blood Teacher

Miss Drak's on 'blood teacher' duty this week.
It's her job to staunch cuts and grazes.
The other teachers hate mopping-up blood
But Miss Drak's fervour amazes.

When you knock on the Staffroom
    door and gasp,
'Playground accident! It's Anne-Marie!'
Miss Drak leaps up and comes running at once.
On her face a look of sheer glee.

She licks her red lips and sets straight to work
Dab dabbing blood from Anne-Marie's chin.
Awestruck we notice Miss Drak has two fangs
And a fiendishly devilish grin.

Wes Magee

Supermiss!

Miss Morris is mild, Miss Morris is meek,
She loves teaching history – Roman and Greek,
She knows all the wars with the French and the
   Spanish,
But when danger threatens, Miss Morris will vanish!
She'll dash, in a flash, to the ladies' staff loo,
Then emerge, in an instant, as somebody new!
Helmeted, caped, in an aura of light,
And with gold-coloured pants that are far, far too
   tight.
With a leap she will launch herself into the air,
And bullies and baddies had better beware!

Supermiss! Supermiss! Classroom crusader!
There's nowhere to hide, villains just can't evade her.
She'll teach them a lesson they'd rather not know.
Now get on with your work, she'll be back in a mo.

There's a sound far away, like a faint thunder-clap
And the sky's punctuated with 'Pow!' and 'Kerzap!'
The occasional 'Whammo!', an 'Unghhh!' or a
    'Wheee!'
And then it goes quiet, as quiet can be.
She lands like a lark, hardly bending the grass,
And in less than a minute is back with her class,
Where Miss Morris says, 'Settle down now! Pay
    attention!
Who knows Galileo's most famous invention?'

Supermiss! Supermiss! Hear the class roar!
But if there's one Supermiss could there be more?
So watch when your teacher pops into the loo.
She just might emerge as a Supermiss too!

Paul Bright

Secret Staffroom

In the close, secret dark of the staffroom,
Early, at break of the day,
There are wild howls and yells,
And most terrible smells.
'Tis teachers at wild, wicked play!

The Head is in charge. He's waving a cane.
What are they up to? What fills me with fear?
Holding hands in a ring,
They're beginning to sing.
I can just hear the word 'disappear'.

There's a pan on the floor of the staffroom.
The teachers are throwing things in.
Pencil-shavings, old pens,
A fragment of lens,
The contents of our litter bin.

There's a sole from a discarded plimsoll,
Some chewing gum scraped from the floor,
Cheesy socks, mouldy chips,
Cat hairs, orange pips,
Horrible garbage galore!

And now the song's words grow much clearer.
I know why these teachers are here!
This terrible smell
Is because of their spell.
It's designed to make kids disappear!

John Kitching

Hidden Depths

Imagine my surprise –
my eyes had trouble believing,
there on the TV screen –
my teacher, stretching and breathing.

He looked almost bald,
his hair was pushed under a cap.
He dived in the water, he was off like a shot,
swimming lap after lap after lap.

He wasn't the fastest, I'll give you that,
but I had him down for a Zimmer.
I couldn't have been more completely wrong,
Mr Smith is an Olympic swimmer!

Chrissie Gittins

Double-Fault

Poor Mrs Johnson's in terrible pain,
she just had to take the day off, once again;
incredibly, when I watched *Tennis Report*;
there was her double, front row, Centre Court.

Mike Johnson

New Neighbours

Living next door to my head teacher
isn't easy.

I couldn't believe it when he moved in
Mum laughed, said it didn't matter
I only had Year Six to go
so what?

I can still hear him
booming out all over the garden
as he tells the bushes off for being untidy
shouts at the flowers to stand up straight
yells at the starlings to sing in tune
commands the lawn to get itself cut
gives the sparrows lines for being cheeky.

Yesterday I felt
his bulging eyes stare at me and Smigsy
playing football in the garden.
He disallowed three of my goals
sent Smigsy home for answering back
then he confiscated our ball
when it bounced on his head
and flattened his hollyhocks.

Mum says I'm over-reacting
it's not all that bad, and if he has banned me
from riding my bike outside his front window
it'll teach me a lesson in manners.

She must be joking, and what's worse
is that the house on the other side is up for sale
and we've been told
the senior dinner lady is going to live there.
Mum, please when can we move?
I can't take much more of this.

David Harmer

Staffroom in the Sky

What in heaven do they talk about,
Old teachers when they die,
Sitting around and sipping tea
In that Staffroom in the Sky?

Oh, they talk of old days at the chalkface,
Of head teachers they loved – or hated,
And the careers of pupils of long ago
Are compared and hotly debated:
There were those who rose to be judges
And others who ended in jail,
One who played soccer for England
And one who just played for Rochdale.
They speak of when things were perfect –
Education's Golden Age –
And that was, of course, for all of them
When *they* were centre stage.
They'll ramble on into Eternity
Repeating their long monologues
And they won't fail to tell
How, since they left the scene,
Everything's gone to the dogs.

Eric Finney

High Flyers

We thought our teacher was ordinary,
we thought she was really boring,
she always looked tired from teaching us
and at weekends was probably snoring.
We thought she led a quiet life
at home, feet up, being lazy,
but it seemed that our teacher had always wanted
to try something really crazy . . .

She told us all in the middle of Maths
she'd be doing a bungee jump,
and we were appalled, we could see her
hitting the ground with a mighty thump.
We were worried it wouldn't be anything else
but one hundred per cent disaster,
our teacher laid out in a hospital bed
with both of her legs in plaster.

She'd be raising lots of money, she said,
for her favourite charity,
but we felt it would all be far too much
for a woman of fifty-three.
Then she said, 'I hope you'll support me,
I expect you all to be there.
It's Saturday afternoon at three,
halfway through our village fair.'

So we all turned up and had to admit
our teacher looked fantastic,
and we watched amazed as she bounced around
on the end of a length of elastic.
She was kitted out in a jumpsuit
that was zigzag yellow and black
and reminded us all of an angry wasp
that was moving in to attack.

But that wasn't the only surprise of the day
because tumbling down from the sky
was a team of freefall divers
who we couldn't identify,
till their parachutes suddenly blossomed
and somebody started to laugh,
when drifting gently down to earth
came the rest of our school staff!

Brian Moses

Mr McConn's Secret

What on earth is the matter with Mr McConn –
he used to look so neat and cool
but now he staggers into school
with a crumpled suit and odd socks on.

His carefree boyish charm has gone,
his worn out baggy eyes are bloodshot,
he's become a raggedy, mumbling clot
who's nodding off all day long.

His aftershave smells more milk than lemon
and on the shoulder of his jacket
is a sticky off-white smear that
has a slighty sickly pong . . .

what on earth is wrong
with Mr McConn?

Dave Calder

Our New Headmaster

Our new Headmaster – Mr C Rocodile
has a smile that's a mile wide.
He always seems cheerful,
keeps his chin and tail up
and certainly gets his teeth into his work.
He comes from foreign climates
and therefore looks rather tanned
as well as thick-skinned.
But I suppose he has to be –
after all he *is* the Headmaster!

He enjoys swimming and music (especially scales)
and, occasionally, when it is very hot
he likes to have a little afternoon nap
where he sleeps like a log!
But one thing to remember
that's worthwhile,
and that is you must never rile
our Mr C Rocodile!
For he has a snappy temper
and if you're very naughty
he'll just simply
bite your head off!

Ian Souter

Teachers' Holidays

Mr Mason flies
to Tenerife. Lies
lazy in the sun.
Eats out, no grief.

The Head would
rather exercise.
Climbing mountains
under cloudy skies.

Mrs Clancy's family
goes to France.
Camping.
Nothing fancy.

Bognor's Mrs Major's
destination.
(Not gifted with
imagination.)

But our Miss Drew!
Backpacks her way to
distant Kathmandu.
Wish we could too!

Ann Bonner

Blackmail

On holiday, my sister,
my mum, my dad and I
were walking down the beach
beneath the Spanish sky
when all at once I saw my teacher
(a horrible surprise)
and my teacher saw me too,
horror in her eyes
and grabbed a handy beach towel,
letting out a screech
for she'd been caught out topless,
topless on the beach.
As we walked away I gloated.
There was little need to mention
that in future she'd think twice
before giving me detention.

Marian Swinger

Our Teacher Has Us Worried

Our teacher has us worried.
We're sure she is going bats!
Her world revolves around those furry creatures
known as CATS.

At home they seem to rule her life.
It's just as well she's no one's wife!

Thirty cats she keeps as pets.
She's told us often, over and over.
We know their names by heart.
There's Trixie, Yoohoo,
Inkpot, Kung-fu,
Claws and Clover,
and that's just six for a start.

For Maths she gives us sums to do
like fifty cans of PUSSY-DINS
@ one pound twenty-seven pence,
plus condensed milk in litre tins –
a weekly bill that's quite immense.

Our stories, when we read or write,
must be of moggies, black and white,
or ginger, tabby, smoky grey.
We even model them in clay.

In Art we always have to draw and
  paint the things.
That's true!
I went real wild today and drew
a cat with butterfly-like wings,
big boots and flowing cape.
But when Miss came and saw my work
she blew a fuse, she went berserk,
right off her trolley, round the twist, and ape.

Then in the corridor, at break,
she purred when Mr Timms went by.
He's got long whiskers,
big green eyes and pointed ears.
Maybe that's why.

And then, at end of school today,
we had a shock as we prepared to troop away.
Miss sprang up on a cupboard top,
and curled up small,
her arms crossed underneath her chin,
so neat and tidy,
giving us a sort of feline grin as out we hurried,
thankful it was Frid'y!

Oh yes!
Our teacher's *really* got us worried.

Barry Buckingham

A Change of Gear

Just clock our teacher,
In town with her bloke:
Cuddling and kissing,
Sharing a Coke.
She looks pretty gorgeous:
Short skirt, cocky hat
And her hair hanging loose –
It's lovely like that.
And the rest of her gear,
Real trendy and cool –
Not quite the kit
She turns up in for school.
Is it her? Look again . . .
Can't believe what I'm seeing:
Our teacher – looking just like
A human being!

Eric Finney

Little but Lethal

Her name is Miss Neil, she's a teacher at school,
She takes us for English and Maths.
She's mousy and timid and quiet and small,
And we mess her around just for laughs.

So how can it be that somebody so small,
And in a 'respectable job',
So quiet and mousy and timid and such
Is really a FOOTBALL YOB???

I couldn't believe it when I found out –
I'd gone to a match with a friend,
A birthday treat – Man U versus Leeds,
We sat at the Stretford Road end.

A Leeds defender had handled the ball,
And the crowd and the players all appealed,
But the ref waved 'play on' and ignored all
    their cries –
It was then that I spotted Miss Neil.

A woman erupted a few seats along,
With red and white stripes on her face,
Green spiky hair and a ring through her nose,
And tattoos all over the place.

She yelled and she screamed and she jumped
    and she waved,
And started a one-woman riot.
And guess who it was – Little Miss Neil,
Who I knew as mousy and quiet!

The police were sent in and they marched her away –
She screamed and she yelled and she fought.
I stood and I stared and I just rubbed my eyes –
That Miss Neil isn't quite what we'd thought!

And in school assembly on Monday morning
The head teacher said, 'By the way,
I will be taking Miss Neil's class for Maths,
I don't think we'll see her today.

I've just had a phone call, she didn't sound good,
She says she's not feeling too well.'
I thought, 'Not surprising, if only he knew –
She'll be still cooling off in a cell . . . '

Clive Webster

Our Head Teacher

Our head teacher has tattoos on his chest,
he's a biker and biking's what he does best.
he's a T.T. rider heading out to the races
with a huge machine to put through its paces.

We imagine him down at the transport caff
talking torque and saying, 'Cars are naff!'
Nothing can beat a run on two wheels
with the wind in his face and tyres that squeal.

He'll tank up and ton up all down the strip,
of all head teachers he's definitely hip.
There's always been a zing in his step
but biking has given him extra pep.

He's easy riding a part in a movie
back when things were fab, gear and groovy,
biking the highways, chasing a dream,
proving that no one is quite what they seem.

He's a biker and biking's what he does best,
yes, our head teacher stands out from the rest.

Brian Moses

Strange Change

Miss Savage isn't herself today,
The Miss we know has faded away –

And in her place is a stranger who
Makes mistakes, and hasn't a clue

How to frighten her class at all,
She's suddenly shy and suddenly small,

She fumbles with sums in Numeracy Hour,
Her shouts are feeble without any power,

Miss Savage has changed – and by the way
The School Inspectors are here today.

Clare Bevan

Meet the Head

Our Head is short and hairy,
His eyes don't miss a thing.
They stare and glint and flash at you,
From side to side they swing.

He lopes around the corridors
And peers through classroom doors.
The staff jump to attention
When he claps his sweaty paws

And if you're misbehaving,
You'd better leg it quick
Before a wiry arm shoots out,
Before you're in his grip.

He likes to show that he's in charge,
He thrusts his chest right out.
And if someone disagrees with him
He splutters, screams and shouts.

We've even seen him stamp his feet
And snarl ferociously.
Our Head is something else, you bet.
Our Head's a chimpanzee!

Patricia Leighton

A History Teacher's Love Song

I love you like Mark Antony
Adored his Cleopatra.
I want us to spend breaktime in
Ancient Egyptian rapture.

I love you like Sir Launcelot
Adored Queen Guinevere.
Romance me like a noble knight
When we get out of here.

I love you like Henry VIII
Adored young Anne Boleyn.
Please woo me with a Tudor rose
When holidays begin.

I love you like Paris loved Helen,
Many years BC,
Tell me you'd launch a thousand ships
Just to be close to me.

I love you with the steady flame
With which Queen Vic loved Albert.
Come find a cosy staffroom chair –
We'll snuggle up in comfort.

I love you like Edward VIII
Adored his Mrs Simpson.
Tell me you'd abdicate for me
And make my cheeks burn crimson.

I love you like Charles number two
Adored actress Nell Gwyn.
Come and perform a play with me
To drown the playground din.

And I love you like Nelson loved
His Lady Hamilton.
Come sail with me through history
When all these kids have gone.

Julia Rawlinson

Tell Telling

Sir's crazy about Switzerland:
he loves to ski
likes cuckoo clocks
and yodels down the corridor.
(He gave Miss Simpkins boxed Swiss
    chocs.)

He tells us about William Tell.
'A hero, bold and
brave,' Sir said:
but now I think he's gone too far.
Help. Get this apple off my head!

Mike Johnson

Calling All Teachers

Is your class unruly?
Is homework never done?
Then call for Superteacher.
Like a bullet from a gun
he will fly to where there's trouble
in his mortar board and gown,
T for teacher on his breast
and on his brow, a frown.
The cheekiest of pupils
fear his X-ray eye,
cowering in corners
as he hurtles through the sky.
Bullies cringe and quiver,
slackers grab their books
and female teachers swoon
before his superhero looks.
He knows what kids are plotting
and his kids control device
makes them do their homework
not just once but twice
and for kids who aren't so clever
there's his brain upgrade (no sham)
where he painlessly inserts
a few more megabytes of ram.

So if your nerves are shredded
and you want to run away,
call for Superteacher
and go on holiday.

Marian Swinger

Colour Code

When she's grumpy,
Wrong side of the bed,
Our teacher wears red.

When she's dreamy,
Too good to be true,
Our teacher wears blue.

When she's rumpled,
Not fit to be seen,
Our teacher wears green.

When she's spiky,
Looking for a fight,
Our teacher wears white.

When she's weary,
A little bit down,
Our teacher wears brown.

When she's bouncy,
Back on the track,
Our teacher wears black.

When she's at home,
Singing at the sink,
Our teacher wears frilly, silly,
        straight-from-the-skating-rink,
Twinkly, crinkly, who-cares-what-
        people-think,
PINK!!!

Clare Bevan

Mr Fledermaus

Our teacher, Mr Fledermaus, seems frightened
  of the light,
He comes to school before the dawn,
  and goes home late at night.
His face is almost deathly pale; he wears
  a long black cloak,
And with those little pointed teeth he really
  looks a joke.
He ought to eat much more, he should put
  on a bit of weight,
But he left the garlic mushrooms in a pile
  upon his plate.
He often nips into the loo, to comb his sleek,
  black hair,
But they say that, in the mirror, no reflection
  greets him there!
The weirdest things upset him, like that time
  the other day
I was sharpening my pencil, and he winced,
  and looked away.
I think Miss Cartwright fancies him, and
  though she's quite a wreck,
He does seem strangely taken with her long
  and shapely neck!

Paul Bright

The Horrible Headmonster

A new Headmaster arrives next week
  and rumours about him are rife.
They say he growls like a grizzly bear
  and that he chopped up his wife.

It's said he'll stride and stomp around school
  like a zombie in the night,
and that his icicle stare can freeze
  hundreds of children with fright.

It's rumoured he wears a skull-shaped ring,
   and a tie with nests of fleas.
When he smiles he shows razor-sharp fangs.
   There are tattoos on his knees.

We've heard that he has a werewolf's howl.
   There's a jagged scar on his cheek.
They say that he owns a whippy cane
   and that he'll use it next week.

Already he's called 'The Headmonster',
   and some have named him 'The Ghoul'.
We'll know next week if the rumours are true
   when he arrives at our school.

Wes Magee

The Escape Club

There were teachers round the table,
There were teachers up the stairs
There were teachers piled in
  heaps up on the chairs.

There were teachers looking hopeful,
There were teachers turning grey,
There were one or two whose minds had gone astray.

But all of them held something
In their hand or on their lap,
A shovel or a bucket or a map,

And some wore false moustaches,
And some were in disguise
As movie stars with shades to hide their eyes,

And one had dug a tunnel,
And one had built a boat,
(If the staffroom ever flooded it would float),

And one had made a glider
Out of yogurt pots and string,
(Though nobody was keen to fly the thing.)

They discussed the best escape routes
From the classroom and the hall,
They chalked their latest plans along the wall,

They talked about a future
Far from paperwork and stress,
From lessons and from registers and mess.

No nasty heaps or marking,
No musty cloakroom smells,
No playground duties, no more clanging bells.

Then they heard a whistle shrieking
And the meeting closed in gloom
As the teachers sadly shuffled from the room.

But if you spot a scraping noise
Beneath your classroom floor,
Or a silent stranger scuttles past the door,

Or if you find a cupboard
Packed with parachutes and rope,
Then you'll know that teachers
   never give up hope!

Clare Bevan

A Teacher of Many Parts

We learned, half-term, our Miss Maclean's
An actress on our TV screens,
In ads, it's true, she mainly is
But all the same – she's in showbiz!

Rebecca says she's seen her hand
Act with soap of a well-known brand
And Sharon recognized her teeth
And knew the nose they flashed beneath.

And Pauline's sure, and Den and Brad,
Her left ear stars in this eardrops ad,
And Lauren thinks she's seen her hair
Wearing gel – though she couldn't swear.

So first day back, excitedly,
We're crowding our celebrity –
Our teacher's really won our hearts
With her many famous parts!

Philip Waddell

Something Up With Miss

There's something up with our teacher today
And we think it's our fault
We sit quietly for the register
And not even Sonia calls out.
We pick up our maths books
Without the usual fuss
And work with our heads down.

Peeping over our arms
We watch her
Sitting at her desk,
Not gliding round the room.
She sniffs
And the room goes so silent
We all hear that one tear drop
Plop on her mark book.

When we have troubles
We go straight to teacher for help
But where do teachers go when they are upset?
Today, no one in our class has a problem.
We get on with our work without complaint.

John Coldwell

Our Teacher is Really from Outer Space

Early morning he lands his spaceship
behind the boilers where nobody goes
then he wobbles across the yard
his bright purple hair glowing with sparks
his six eyes standing out on stalks
his fifteen arms ending in claws
his four mouths drooling orange spit.

Once inside he pops to the gents
changes into his Earthling Teacher Disguise
hairy tweed jacket and scrawny tie
saggy trousers with a shiny bottom
squeaky shoes and a smell of chalkdust.

Sometimes in Maths
he forgets where he is, starts scribbling
strange signs and numbers across the board
mutters and snorts in some weird language
his antennae nearly zoom up through his wig
his alien face peers through his mask.

In PE he sprouts ten legs
does tricks with a football you wouldn't believe
and luckily for us, at dinner time
he is a vegetarian.

After school when he thinks we can't see
he blasts off home to the faraway stars
with our homework under his arms
just think, it could be
he has friends in lots of
  other schools.

Next time you're in assembly
take a long look and try to guess
which ones are the teachers from
  outer space.
They could be nearer than
  you think.

David Harmer

The Gizmo Master

We had a sort of weirdo
come and teach our class last week.
All weedy thin and gangly,
softly spoken, pale and meek.
We thought we'd play him up no end,
and treat him really rotten,
but all our sly and wicked plans
were very soon forgotten.

He showed the class a gizmo –
said he'd had it many years.
He called it a 'Reducer' and,
ignoring all our sneers,
he focused it, he tuned it,
pressed a button in a socket,
then shrank a chair to mini-size
and popped it in his pocket.

At breaktime, Andy, Paul and I
all had a little natter.
We think he's from the future,
which is quite a serious matter.
Perhaps he's met Duck Rogers,
Captain Shirt and Mr Sok.
But we'll be telling no-one else –
they'd say it's poppycock!

So if *you* get a teacher
who looks weird and pale and meek,
think twice before you play him up.
Don't give him any cheek.
He could be like *our* teacher,
from the future in disguise.
He might whip out a gizmo . . .
and you'll end up mini-size.

Barry Buckingham

A Teacher of Habit

Each day,
at 7.30 precisely,
Mr Talbot (Maths),
man of few words
but many figures,
arrives at school.
Mr Talbot (Maths), man of apparently no
sense of humour and never known to
take a day off sick, can be relied upon
not only for his punctuality but also to
turn up, always in the same smart, met-
tallic grey suit. Mr Talbot (Maths) teaches his subject with the smoothness of a
well oiled machine, turning out, year
after year, perfectly tutored pupils. Then,
at the end of each well-run day, with
never the smallest change to his routine,
Mr Talbot (Maths), teacher of habit,
departs the school, not a second before,
not a second after, the stroke of 5.00.
Though highly respected, his colleagues
think Mr Talbot   (Maths) is some-
what obsessed   by his subject
but that is be-   cause none have
ever seen him   at home in the
evening. If they   did they would
be surprised   to see that the
s e c o n d   M r   Talbot (Maths)
shuts his front   door behind him,
this model   teacher re-
charges his   batteries by
switching off   completely.

Philip Waddell

Miss Carter Could Once Have Been Married

Miss Carter could once have been married,
But she stayed home to look after her mum;
By the time she was fifty-seven,
She thought that her chances had gone.

Now Miss Carter fancied the lollipop man;
He waved, and *she* smiled, every day
As she drove her car through the school gates,
But never a word did they say.

Yes, Miss Carter she fancied the lollipop man,
But she never thought they would meet;
Till, one day, she decided to walk to school,
And he helped her across the street.

Well, that was all that they needed.
They both retired after that.
And they opened a shop in St Leonards-on-Sea,
Selling lollipops and funny hats.

Mike Jubb

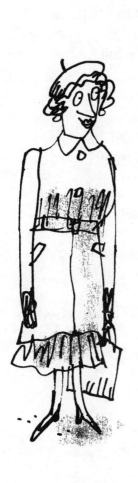
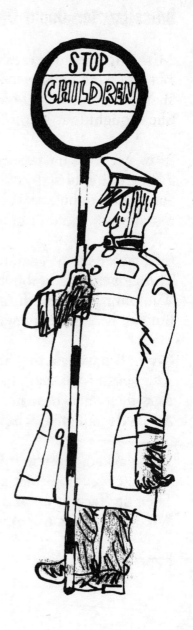

Our New Teacher

Last Christmas our teacher went skiing
Leaping from glaciers with glee
She zoomed down ravines like a champion
But she couldn't get on with 6B

At Easter she sailed around Iceland
Pitting her wits 'gainst the sea
She rode the huge waves single-handed
But she just couldn't handle 6B

In summer she went pony-trekking
Through the wild mountain ranges of Chile
Went white-water rafting in a tiny canoe
But she couldn't cope with 6B

Now 6B have left for the big school
And teacher has us in her charge
And we love to hear her adventures
And we're all well behaved – by and large

So we asked, Do you miss your old class, Miss?
And she went all quiet and sad
Then her face lit up and she started to laugh.
What, me? Miss 6B? Are you mad?

Roger Stevens

Mrs Tompkins Won't Tell

Mrs Tomkins plays the piano,
Has permed hair and does supply.
During term she seems quite boring,
Unexceptional and shy.

Unbeknown to all her pupils,
Unsuspected by the staff,
Billy Baxter's Mum's her cleaner,
She has seen *THE PHOTOGRAPH!*

Dressed in shorts and stretchy sun-top,
In a hotel far from Peckham
Mrs T. beams, bold and buxom,
With her arms round David Beckham!

Just a holiday encounter
With the World Cup England team,
Mrs T. explained when challenged,
But in her eye, a lingering gleam.

No one knows what really happened,
Or if a romance flourished since.
The Secret Life of Mrs Tomkins
Stays safe beneath the pale blue rinse.

Daphne Kitching

The Hypnoteacher

Our teacher is a hypnotist
He puts us in a trance
We stand still in the playground
In the hall he makes us dance

Our Head is totally amazed
That our classroom is so quiet
Because our class is 6B
And it used to be a riot

Our classroom's full of paintings
Display work everywhere
Charts and maps and poetry
Cover ceilings, walls and chair

We can say our eight-times table
Computers – we know each feature
We can recite all Shakespeare's plays
Thanks to our hypnoteacher

But every day at half-past three
When the school bell starts to ring
His fingers click – we all wake up
And can't remember a thing

Roger Stevens

Cyber Love

Miss Smith is in love with an email man;
she writes to him every night.
And though he lives across the world,
it was always love at first write.

She sits there at her computer
to tell him how much she cares;
and how she's been saving up for a trip
to visit him out there.

And *he* writes back to tell her
that his love will always be true;
but maybe staying at home for now
would be the sensible thing to do.

Miss Smith will have a terrible shock,
if she meets her email mate,
because *she* was twenty-five last week,
and *he's* nearly ninety-eight.

Mike Jubb

Geography Lesson

Our teacher told us one day he would leave
And sail across a warm blue sea
To places he had only known from maps,
And all his life had longed to be.

The house he lived in was narrow and grey
But in his mind's eye he could see
Sweet-scented jasmine clinging to the walls,
And green leaves burning on an orange tree.

He spoke of the lands he longed to visit,
Where it was never drab or cold.
I couldn't understand why he never left,
And shook off the school's stranglehold.

Then halfway through his final term
He took ill and never returned.
He never got to that place on the map
Where the green leaves of the orange trees burned.

The maps were redrawn on the classroom wall;
His name forgotten, he faded away.
But a lesson he never knew he taught
Is with me to this day.

I travel to where the green leaves burn,
To where the ocean's glass-clear and blue,
To places our teacher taught me to love –
And which he never knew.

Brian Patten

Retiring

Our teacher, Mrs Batlow
is leaving this week,
after 40 years of teaching.
So on Friday all of Class 5W
give her a present.
Most of us give her a card
with '*best wishes*' but
Sarah presents her with a painting
of Mrs Batlow standing in front of the school.
Emily gives her some flowers.
Nathan gives her a box of chocolates.
Lorenzo gives her a framed photo of Class 5W.
Penny gives her a box of apples!
(Penny's Dad owns a fruit shop.)
Simon gives her a pen in a special case.

Mrs Batlow smiles at each present
and thanks every child
but when Peter gives her his homework
all finished, neat and tidy,
for the first time this year
we all notice that
Mrs Batlow is crying
but
we're not sure if she's happy
or
if she's crying because
she has to mark Peter's homework.

Steven Herrick

THE TEACHER'S REVENGE

Poems chosen by Brian Moses

In an average classroom, in an average town, on an average afternoon it is not only the pupils who are staring at the clock longing for the bell to ring. The teachers are waiting too . . . An anthology of poems that reveal exactly what teachers would really, really like to do to their pupils if they could! Peek inside the staffroom and discover the secret dreams and horrible intents that lurk there – if you dare!

The Pupil Control Gadget

Science teacher Robert West
built a gadget, which, when pressed
caused consternation far and wide
by zapping pupils in mid-stride.
It froze all motion, stopped all noise,
controlled the rowdy girls and boys,
and on fast forward was great fun.
It made them get their schoolwork done,
their hands a blur, their paper smoking,
with teachers cheering, laughing, joking.
And on rewind (that too was nice),
you could make them do their schoolwork twice.
Robert, now a millionaire,
is selling gadgets everywhere.
Timid teachers, pupil bossed
pay cash and never mind the cost.

Marian Swinger

Who Rules the School?

Poems chosen by Paul Cookson

The Beast on Dinner Time Duty

The dinner line was single file
With no one allowed to speak,
And if you did you were sent to the back
Of the line for the rest of the week.

She didn't like conkers or marbles
and playground footy was banned,
and if you were caught she'd take the ball
and burst it with one of her hands.

Everyone eats up their cabbage,
no one leaves anything green.
She's the Frankenstein of the food hall,
the King Kong of the canteen.

A beast on dinner time duty,
a roar that causes earthquakes.
Children shiver, teachers tremble
and even the headmaster shakes.

A dinosaur in the dining room,
prehistoric, unfeasibly large.
Who rules the school? Don't be a fool!
She's the one that's in charge.

Paul Cookson

Who Rules the School Now?

Poems chosen by Paul Cookson

An uproarious book of poems about power struggles within a school. Who really rules the school? The pupils, the dinner ladies, the secretary – or maybe something else altogether? They all have their story to tell . . .

from
The Arrogant Fire Alarm

They shut me in a glass prison – the fools.
But even here
I rule this school
And all must obey me
Without question.

John Coldwell

Spectacular Schools

Poems chosen by
Paul Cookson and David Harmer

Sneak a peek into the craziest classrooms ever! Find out what snowmen learn, and sing the dragon school song. Discover how to become a pirate, and which vampire school to choose. You'll never look at your own school in the same way again!

from

Circus School Reception Class

My little brother Adam
has started circus school.

He's learning to juggle two teddy bears
and to throw rubber knives at a wooden man.

For homework he balanced
Mum and Grandma on his head.

Next year he's in Year One
doing lion taming.

David Harmer

How To Embarrass Grown-Ups

Poems chosen by Paul Cookson

Ever wanted to get your own back on grown-ups? Ever cringed at something your parents or teachers have done? Then these poems are for you! Packed full of embarrassing situations, they are funny, rude and very useful . . . Be warned – they'll make you squirm!

from

Dad's Birthday Gift

Every year
We go to Gran's for birthday tea.
Every year
Dad shows off the new tie.
Every year
Gran says,
'I never know what to buy you.'
Every year
Dad says,
'You can never have enough ties.'

But this year
My little brother says,
'Gran, is your cat feeling better?
Because Dad said it had been sick on his new tie.'

John Coldwell